# Aether

Xavier Yeldell

"There are some things one can only achieve by a deliberate leap
in the opposite direction." – **Franz Kafka**

# Contents

# I – Appreciation

## Present

My name isn't essential.

I don't know what I am, really.

Walking and writing have become two avenues

For me to improve my awareness,

And yet I still find myself stuck to moments in time.

It's difficult to take control of these forces while balancing

The complexities of the world I was thrown into.

I didn't ask to be immobile and withdraw into corners of scare peace.

With all of these thoughts that push against my head,

I suppose sharing them is worthwhile.

# The Home

Of a lone wanderer is never settled,

Like the existentialism that cycles my headspace.

I let acoustic strings control my breathing

And focus on rippling waters,

Daydreaming about the faith I lost years ago.

When curious crawlers interact with me,

I think about the spectrum of power between us.

Evident contrast, innocence compared.

My omnipotence was light, however,

So I chose to not displace them.

Sometimes the wind will tickle my concentration

And remind me to move,

But it can't seem to change my stagnancy.

Often I feel my fingers seeping into the green beneath,

Urging me to remain with them.

Sometimes I overthink,

And even when clarity stares at my somber face in patience,

I put a paper bag over it.

# Nirvana

Translucent waves skim across

My feet with sincerity while

Rinsing smooth stones next to me.

A gentle blaze of the sun beaming my body caringly

As a melody holds this nirvana stable.

This abundant render, produced by my imagination,

Makes escaping a little easier.

# Blue

Vast, vigorous,

Swallowing my spirit and will with ease.

Exquisite, magical,

She pins at my eyes but flows on my tongue.

Her teases provoke me to comply.

Floating through,

Pushing me gradually to feel my thoughts,

Learning, empathizing.

She permits me to explore her depths.

I tread carefully, touch delicately,

Sensations ignite and embrace euphoria.

She's healing my scars,

Eradicating my poison.

Rekindled with hope,

Revived anew.

My sweet blue,

May we stay together forever.

# Yellow

Acres that expand across horizons are my desire,

Threading aural love in solidarity

While the soil presses against my soles.

Clouds scattered in the bluest pools,

Daylight beaming atop yellow acres.

Here, I find refuge.

Nights of constant strain drive me here;

They can wash away my stress, my fears.

Nothing will stand in my way

Of wanting a different kind of peace.

# Green

Glistens in sprinkles of dews,

Dampening my ankles lovingly.

I've taken her for granted,

I see that now.

She's given me a chance to redeem myself,

So who am I to oppose the invitation?

## Fluid

Amid these confusing times,

I've managed to walk down

A path cleared for direction.

I find myself seeking desire

In many different forms,

Not just the biological.

Personality and femininity

Are the two main ingredients

For a wonderfully crafted soulmate.

The more I analyze, the more

I shed the roles I was assigned since birth.

I want to wear the universal art

That so many talented beings possess,

To truly express a side of myself

That needs to rise to the surface.

## Perfect Love

My dearest,

May you become the discovery in my lostness,

A soul so beautiful that the sky paints you in its image.

May we settle close with perfect love,

Gazing the nature in front of our glossy eyes

That kindly pour delicate tears.

May your radiating glow secrete perpetually.

May my mind finally rest these recycled, oversaturated thoughts

And subdue itself peacefully.

May our perfect love eradicate our trauma,

Mending our souls into something better, stronger.

May you be my one true perfect love.

# Highs

Pleasure in the wild

Is caught by me,

Used for the day.

I get lifted upwards with rejoice.

Everything is amazing,

Everything is incredible.

Ascension.

# II – Jumbled Nostalgia

# The Highway

Paved my consolation back when things were simple.

I watched it expand for many years,

Challenging the zooms outside the

Red wagon with my keen observation.

The breathing radio was warranted company,

As well as the sky bleeding lustrous colors from storm
aftermaths or mellow dusks.

The highway traced those temporary thoughts

Of mine that breached reality

And kept me distracted.

The highway is etched in my brain,

Reflecting its position on those trips

To the bubbled town of wealth,

Where I fell hypnotic to the sounds of queens.

And on this infinitely charged highway,

My young spirit still rides it.

## That Night on Bonaventure

Where screams of thrill-seekers and kinetic energy

Grasped all of my attention,

And sparked excitement with every step I took.

Stuffed animals, large and ludicrous,

Would cry out for my impulsivity

Until giving in to their pleas.

Splendid ecstasy in sugary proportions

Elevated the already adventurous experience,

Falling over absolute prominence.

# Security

From the scalding overhead,

Splashing from the back and

Through the body.

Echoing melodies;

Feeling, believing,

Grooving as the notes sync with the drops

And I start to mutter a tune.

# Fifteen

Backward in motion

With cotton-blend on my legs

And flaws on my face.


Sweaty palm trees,

Dark mornings,

Pop-rap ringing in both ears.


Tight anxiety,

Friends lost; strangers found.

Noon under pieces of antiquity.


The cold 400s,

The humid 800s,

That one room from the 300s that still wonders where I've been all this time,


And blissful delusion.

## Coffee

Warm blinds from across my room

Bleed over me.

They tell me to wake slowly and

Soak the energy of a rejuvenated Sunday.

An aroma of roasting coffee,

Sizzling margarine,

And sounds of smooth jazz take up the first floor of my home
gracefully.

It's another Sunday that

Calls for relaxation and reflection.

It's another Sunday that

Descends me into pure leisure

While skimming through the funny pages,

Settling on my perfect sofa and letting the fabric

Sink into my skin.

It's another new Sunday that

Allows me to smell the roasting coffee,

Sizzling margarine,

And sounds of smooth jazz that whistle through my old soul.

# Elsewhere

Lies a sacred place

Where my company is valued.

Golden hour,

Walking through pieces of

Abstract memory and tangibility.

Looking in all directions, observing forever

At golden hour, alone.

An institution of the past,

It means something to me, elsewhere.

My affection for the mundane is endearing,

It's progressed in interesting aspects.

Elsewhere lies this realm that

Captures itself for my own pleasure,

Speaking volumes while projecting

A protected plain for me to explore.

# Sixteen

Change was pending

With enough confusion to

Focus on the wrong things, the wrong people.


Pop-rap still ringing,

But then came alternative

And rock, the unlikely heroes.


School glistened on

The late afternoons,

Empty courts swarming with generous tranquility.


Emotions were aggressively thrown,

Tackled with deception.

Cabin fever caved in with demonic roommates who teased

And overstayed their welcome.


This wasn't blissful, but I was still deluded.

# Queens

Of influence and stardom,

Saving me with their voices as a child.

It was Gaga,

Katy,

Riri,

Kesha,

Nicki,

Demi,

Selena,

Lorde,

Hayley,

And Ari,

Suppressing my struggles with their art,

Forever grateful for the exposure.

# Dreamscape

A wavelength of hypnotism

With a foreign light,

Is powered by sentiment.

I've kept this mystical being close for years,

Studying its power and grace,

Understanding my fascination with it.

I believe it was born in another world,

One of supreme sophistication.

As the being moves throughout space and time,

Its influence is peppered across the cosmos.

Iridescent colors bloom on its body,

As it sings brilliantly without worry.

# The Room

Was bright with colors on the floor and walls.

Knees scrapping over foam and carpet,

Careless of the soft rain outside.

It was cold in the room,

And I didn't have a jacket with me.

Amid the activity,

I found it easier to follow the moving pictures

Playing on the goliath,

Munching on something routine and processed.

The room had his invisible, intangible

Powcr to its structure.

I couldn't figure it out 'cos

It was cold in the room,

And I didn't have a jacket with me.

## Seventeen

Lost boy, beaten.

Grabbed by the throat,

Thrown off a terrace.


Menacing vipers,

Striking faux love

That tenderizes the heart.


Drowning in the dry,

Melting under heat

With dirty onlookers.


Punishments weren't necessary,

And yet, I obliged.

Ingrained anguish,

Hidden under a hat and hoodie

As a disguise.

# III – Spiral into Madness

# Forgetful

Perpetual stimuli,

Floods of the past,

They never vanish.

It's deteriorating my mind.

I can't truly forget,

And that's what's killing me.

# I'm Content

With feeling this new wave of severance.

I still hold love for the lost ones,

Even if I'm not receiving the same amount in return.

I'm content with the walls that divide my past into three slices of affliction,

Teasing me to break through with every memory that I reproduce.

I'm content with continuously lying to myself.

I'm content with adding more pain to carry,

Climbing mountains of fallacy until I bleed

From my hardened hands and release in defeat.

**Delivered**

Hey

...

*Hey*

How are you?

...

*I'm good U?*

Yeah, same here

So I kinda wanted to talk to you about something

...

You there?

...

*I'm busy rn*

Oh okay

I just wanted to tell you that I like you a lot

Ik it's out of nowhere byt I wanted to bring it up

But*

...

Maybe I shouldn't have said anything

...

I just couldn't hold it in anymore

You're beautiful and amazing and gorgeous

I'm not like those other guys, I care about you a lot

…

I think I messed things up

I keep overthingking

Overthinking*

Would you be up to maybe going out sometime?

…

Please say something

Ik you're busy but please

…

Fuck

I shouldn't have said anything

…

Hello?

???

…

(Call Failed)

You know what

Fuck you

I'm done

**Delivered**

## Broward

Fourteen years alienated,

Fourteen years stiffened.

Living in this place hasn't been the same.

Bodies disappeared from me,

Voices devolved into linear screen text.

*"That's just life,"* they say.

I've focused so much of my energy on memories

That they reproduce faster than rabbits.

Marking where this and that happened,

When and with who, is exhausting.

I could be a cartographer for all that I can recall,

I bet it would impress people.

# Responsibility

Saving people of their problems was

Something I thought I could handle.

Once they all scattered across my desk table,

However, suddenly my world wasn't so steady anymore.

I felt like a hero with all the answers,

An invincible beacon of hope.

But beacons don't shine forever,

And in my case, it hasn't stopped shortening out.

## A Picture Can Steal a Thousand Feelings

And host cycles of questions that are left unanswered.

Gray, wispy, unanswered questions floating aimlessly.

I can't push these irritable feelings away

When I look at life without my involvement.

I'm flawed, here's my confession.

I'm trying to run the marathon of transition

But my shoelaces are tied together tightly.

Associations of others puncture at my mind,

Bruising those gray and wispy unanswered questions.

Drowning at my own expense;

Unclear as to what will come of myself,

And unsure if I will ever rest the past

Down in its grave where it belongs.

# Twisted

Lurking through lines,

Beautiful creatures everywhere,

Majestic beings of desire.

I look once, twice,

Every wasted few minutes of my life absorbed by a screen.

Guilt materializes every time.

Obsession, fixation, admiration mutating.

While my control fades, my reality loosens.

We're strangers,

Yet the cinema in my head premieres our special feature,

With me at the front row demanding an encore.

## Addiction

Always pinches away at my nerves

When I can't control my urges.

Lack of intimacy provoked, tugged away

At my sensitive strings.

I needed to release, that's all.

Then came guilty repetition by

Scenes of bodies performing.

How have I cycled myself to this torture?

Why can't I stop?

# Comatose

Some nights I leer at my comforter

And interrogate my pillows

For covering me in perverted dreams.

Tender faces of familiarity come toward me,

Yet I always seem to be out of reach.

They want to me to decipher the messages

As if I can pinpoint a desirable answer,

But it's all scrambled.

Actions shift into rubber and into chaos

Until they force me to open my eyes

To another morning.

## Realm I

I underestimate my subconscious.

The trip I took down to my many realms,

Strange and disorienting.

A woman, a classroom, and it's dark.

There's a gate to another world.

It's hellish.

Attempting to rush in,

Others are negotiating with her,

But she closes the door behind me,

Holding my body with steadfast love.

She tells me that she needs to find them,

And I ask who.

She opens the door and pushes me through it,

Sealing it shut.

I watch her run until her body blended in with the burning scarlet around her.

I underestimate my subconscious.

The trip I took in that realm,

Strange and disorienting.

# Heavy Baggage

Straps around my sore shoulders

With enough weight to crush my bones.

I limp across crowds of oblivious beings,

Wailing for a saint.

I can't take it off,

It's crushing me.

Once they notice my life evaporating,

Collective whispers surround my last moments of consciousness:

"Oh, I'm sorry to hear that."

# Weston

The bubbled town of wealth

Was wide and pampered.

A resident of almost seven years,

Present through trails of thoughts

And adolescent troubles.

Territories held by the White monarchs

And the Latinx royals,

A present inequality of life.

I lived in corners,

Barely scraping by for knowledge.

Living in the wide and pampered bubbled town of wealth

Was a spectacle of false reality.

A clean surface with an undertow of lies and lucrative actions,

Festering across the hills and the falls,

The savanna and the ridges.

I was offered multiple grace periods by my struggles

As compensation for their collateral damage.

There are moments I keep close within,

Making the appropriate tweaks

To form better memories.

In the epilogue I created two plains of my experience;

One of pain and one of peace.

Often these plains collide and implode,

Patching together in a wickedly beautiful collection,

Ricocheting memories until I grow exhausted.

I'm grateful to have left it,

But when I go back, it still bothers me.

Maybe this is one of my unfortunate curses.

# Deceitful

Dead shoes that leave rooms to

The hallways and walkways are compelling.

Plugged dependencies,

Dopamine fixtures.

Brushing through bodies mindlessly, laser focused.

I'm responsible for

Swaying passed friends and enemies,

Just like everyone else.

It's universal, typical.

Eyes can meet but always dash away,

Finding something to avoid the split-second connection of tragic history.

Repressions pour out harder than the occasional rainstorms outside,

Too difficult to control.

Compelling and deceitful dead shoes, leaving rooms

To the hallways and walkways,

Print stories left in their trails.

## One After Another

The conglomerate of rejection

Piles up together like raked autumn leaves.

They stretch across the horizon, one after another.

To these plies of rejection,

I fall into a rampage.

One after another, kicking, swinging, exasperating

All the built-up frustration against those piles.

Depletion couldn't control my anger,

I needed to destroy them until the plain was cleared.

But the rejections just kept piling, one after another.

# Limbo

Awake, again.

Breathing,

Living,

Staring at all my blessings like an ingrate.

Having what others don't,

Why can't I see that?

What's wrong with me?

This four-walled limbo is secretly cutting me open

Every waking day,

Weakness closing in every waking day.

# Realm II

There's a gas station in the middle of nowhere –

Desolate, ominous.

A familiar gang of sleuths is inching closer to it; theme eleven rolls.

A figure, small and wooden, creeps under a light,

Facing an invisible audience with a static yet sinister grin.

His eyes darted from left to right as the theme shook forth.

When it finished, the figure walked away.

Theme eleven is infamous, notorious,

It does away with my vulnerability and triumphs in this realm.

Even with all of that,

I find it too intriguing to repress.

## Restless

With layers of green and brown

Cementing my body in totality.

I'm sinking to the depths of the fabric

With suffocating emotion.

Burn the base,

I need to breathe.

Try to reach in, and you'll suffer a similar fate.

I fear my dreams for their malevolence and mercilessness,

They still swing me across dimensions of people

And places, splats of muddled neon.

*"It's for fun,"* they say,

*"You've been hurting yourself lately, it's our turn."*

Cursing me with agony.

Restless after hours, rotting and absorbing

Harmful radiation.

Sanity dissolving,

Please burn the base before

I finish the job for you.

# Chips

And white strips that

Mock this depression are volatile.

There it is again; it's taking over.

I can't defend myself,

I'm trapped with no escape.

Actions driving a stick shift,

Drifting, tumbling into a flaming fireball.

Chips nudge at my arm,

Begging me to give in.

In seconds, my fingers coat its oil

While my mouth unwillingly dances to its salt.

Flaky, airy, painful.

I keep filling up and breaking down.

There's no end, I have no control.

Boredom is subduing me,

And I'm on the floor filled with more junk than before.

# I'm Done

With blaring all the meaningful words I want,

They'll still produce migraines that follow down to my eyes

On the small screen, cupping my right hand.

Active poisoning, pollution.

These thoughts are rebelling.

Why can't I shut down?

What awaits me on the other side?

A bottle or two, staring at my reduced spirit.

Magnetic seduction;

I'm incinerating my throat,

Inviting the numbness to steal the scraps

While the last of my belief eradicates.

God isn't here, no one is,

And no one ever was.

# Red

And thick crimson

Drips from my forehead.

Shards at the bottom reveal a broken man,

I'm losing it.

Throbbing sensations

Quake within,

Counting the seconds before I fall.

The ugly asphalt provokes the

Thought of a savior,

But I can't hear anything.

The thick crimson expands its volume,

Coating my right side and forming a puddle of pity.

Vision blurry, soul snatched.

It's over.

# Lows

Misery in the wild

Is captured reluctantly,

Used for the night.

Collapsed to the ground

In rapid succession,

Sadness drills through my glass body

As I try to scream with no voice.

Everything is awful,

Everything is terrible.

Descension.

# IV - Salvation

## Nothing

Feels right.

Still breathing, thinking, endlessly.

My eyes are trying to stay open,

My heart is bleeding excessively.

Nothing feels right,

I can't seem to change things.

My fate was never written scripture,

Only words perched in the atmosphere.

# Decisions

Split through time and divide reality.

Decisions carry and shape the world around me,

Weighing down hefty risks.

Doing one thing or the other,

Debating, contemplating.

Who'll be affected?

Responsibility chains me,

And I want to set free.

Instinct, probabilities.

I'm overthinking,

But decisions warrant reactions,

No matter the outcome.

I guess it's fruitless to predict the future,

At least for now.

Decisions need to be tamed, regulated.

Choosing what to do in the space of time,

I need to point to the right ones,

But which are they?

What price do I pay for free will?

## I Can't Please Everyone

I draw my actions with strokes of fatigue,

Shading shapes with only dark colors.

I do what I can,

But I never learn,

And I can't please everyone.

I strive for greatness,

Conditioned to help,

To be human.

I wake up on bright, humid mornings,

In a room of suffocating thoughts with no smile.

I'm my worst critic,

So there's no telling if I can ever please myself.

## Everything Happens for a Reason

I'm on a tightrope with no balance,

Trying to discern how I can consider the past as some blueprint.

Is there some ideal layout for me that I must allow patience to guide me towards?

Frustration is disguised as my bed, wrapping me with fatigue.

Might I withdraw and figure it out,

Or let the universe play its game,

And be content with the course I've been given?

# I Pledge Allegiance

*To the scorched flag,*

*Of the Divided States of AmeriKKKa*

*And to the corrupted Republic,*

*For which it so despairingly stands,*

*One broken nation under no one*

*Very much divisible*

*With no liberty or justice for all.*

## You're Going to Die

Because the truth lies within us all,

Buzzing pointlessly, irritatingly.

It lives in my warped brain,

It lives through my old life,

And it spews over the strangers that I meet.

As a kid,

Everything was a lie.

As a teen,

Everything was a consequence

Now as an adult,

Everything is a revelation.

As my eyes open, anger explodes.

I don't want to exist.

Someone, please save me.

S

       A

           V

              E

                  M

                    E...

# Aether

*I'm*

*here.*

*This*

*is*

*it.*

*I*

*wanted*

*this.*

*I'm*

*finally*

*free*

*of*

*the*

*world*

*below,*

*No*

*longer*

*contained.*

*I*

*can*

*float*

*about,*

*without*

*a*

*thought.*

*Clear*

*mind,*

*calm*

*soul.*

*Pink,*

    *Orange,*

      *Purple,*

        *Such*

          *a*

            *beautiful*

          *confection.*

        *I*

     *wanted*

   *this,*

*Nothing*

   *else.*

    *I've*

      *been*

*saved.*

# I

Can't seem to rest.

Something's troubling me,

What is it?

I hear a voice in my head,

Telling me to come back.

It's relentless,

I listened.

The voice spoke of wisdom,

Expressing reason and understanding,

Wrapped together in empathy.

My body grew warm and bright,

Then I launched downward.

# Am

A cocoon of energy protected my collision,

And from the cinders, I rose.

Maybe I have more time to make things right.

## Reborn

I'm picking up my pieces every day,

Trying to mold back some resemblance of hope.

While the world continues to roll itself in a fire.

I'm still trying to pick up my pieces.

That's all I can really do.

I thought about the easy ways of leaving, I really did.

But that's selfish, too many care and love for me.

I'm picking up my pieces every day.

Eventually, I'll finish,

And then I will be reborn.

End.